Charles Drew
Pioneer in Medicine

Anne Schraff

E

Enslow Publishers, Inc.

40 Industrial Road   PO Box 38
Box 398   Aldershot
Berkeley Heights, NJ 07922   Hants GU12 6BP
USA   UK

http://www.enslow.com

Library of Congress Cataloging-in-Publication Data

Schraff, Anne E.
    Charles Drew : pioneer in medicine / Anne Schraff.
        p. cm. — (Famous inventors)
    Summary: A simple biography of the African American doctor known for his work with blood
plasma.
    Includes index.
    ISBN 0-7660-2008-8
    1. Drew, Charles Richard, 1904–1950—Juvenile literature. 2. Surgeons—United States—
Biography—Juvenile literature. 3. African American surgeons—Biography—Juvenile literature.
4. Blood banks—United States—Juvenile literature. [1. Drew, Charles Richard, 1904–1950.
2. Physicians. 3. African Americans—Biography. 4. Scientists.] I. Title. II. Series.
    RD27.35.D74 S376   2003
    617'.092—dc21

2002010404

To Our Readers:
We have done our best to make sure all Internet Addresses in this book were active and appropriate
when we went to press. However, the author and the publisher have no control over and assume no
liability for the material available on those Internet sites or on other Web sites they may link to. Any
comments or suggestions can be sent by e-mail to comments@enslow.com or to the address on the
back cover.

Every effort has been made to locate all copyright holders of material used in this book. If any errors
or omissions have occurred, corrections will be made in future editions of this book.

Illustration Credits: Moorland-Spingarn Research Center, Howard University, pp. 3, 4, 6, 7, 8, 11, 13,
15, 17, 19, 20, 23, 24, 26; National Archives, p. 28; Stamp Design © U.S. Postal Services. Reproduced
with permission. All rights reserved, p. 27; Library of Congress, p. 21.

Cover Illustration: Moorland-Spingarn Research Center, Howard University

Table of Contents

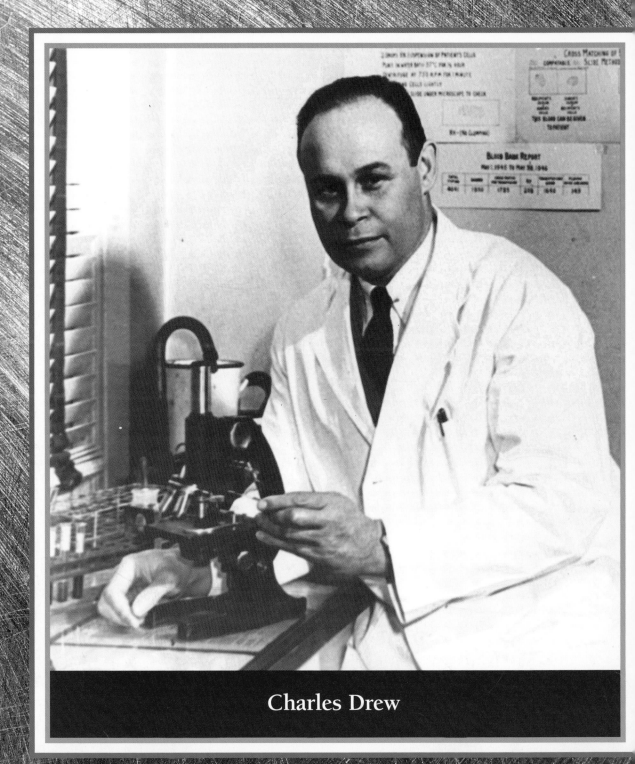

Charles Drew

Chapter 1

A Boy's Dream

When Charles Drew was fourteen years old, his sister Elsie became sick. Everybody was worried. In those days, there were not as many medicines to help people. Elsie got worse and died. She was only twelve years old.

Charles was very sad. He decided then to be a doctor when he grew up. He wanted to save the lives of sick people like his sister Elsie.

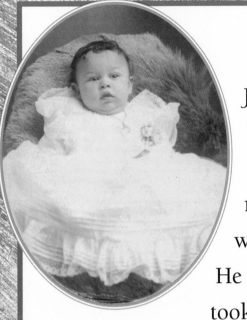

Baby Charles, about six months old.

Charles Richard Drew was born on June 3, 1904, in Washington, D.C. His father, Richard, had a job putting carpets in people's homes. He had never finished high school, but he wanted his children to be educated. He gave them many books to read and took them to museums.

Charles's mother, Nora, had gone to college to become a teacher. When her children were born, she stayed home to care for them. The Drews were a happy family with five children: Charles, Elsie, Joseph, Nora, and Eva.

Charles started school at Stevens Elementary School for black children. White children went to a different school. At that time, black people and white people could not go to school together or work together. Charles was a good student. He liked to play football and basketball. He loved swimming and won many medals.

When Charles was twelve, he took a job selling newspapers on street corners. He had so many papers to sell that he hired other boys to help him. Charles was a good businessman, and he earned money to help his family.

When he was fourteen, Charles went to Dunbar High School for black students. He made fine grades and did well in sports. Charles dreamed of going to college and becoming a doctor. But his family did not have enough money for that. Luckily, Charles was a good

Charles was the eldest child in the family. This photo was taken before Eva was born.

Charles

Joseph

Nora

Elsie

athlete. Perhaps he could get a sports scholarship. A scholarship is money for school.

In 1922, Charles earned a football scholarship to Amherst College in Massachusetts. Amherst College had six hundred students, but only thirteen were African American. It was the first time Charles had ever attended a school with white students. Sometimes he was treated unfairly just because he was African American.

Charles was one of the best players on the college football team. Often, when Amherst played sports against other schools, the crowds were rude. They yelled at the black players. Once, after a big football game, the

Charles in his football uniform.

team decided to eat dinner at a nice hotel. Charles was stopped at the hotel door. *No blacks allowed,* he was told.

Charles was very smart. But he was not asked to join the honor society, a club for Amherst's best students. It was for whites only. Charles was turned away from the college singing club, too. He felt bad about these things. But he did not let them stop him from working hard.

In those days, blacks and whites could not even use the same drinking fountains.

After he finished college, Charles took a job teaching science and coaching sports at Morgan College in Baltimore, Maryland. He saved every penny he could. Finally, he had enough money to begin medical school. He was taking a big step toward his dream of becoming a doctor.

Chapter 2

A Bright Young Doctor

Charles went to McGill Medical School in Montreal, Canada, in 1928. He was far from his family and friends in America. He did not have much money, and sometimes he was lonely in Montreal. He kept his dream of being a doctor always in his mind. It helped him in the hard times.

In 1930, Charles won a Rosenwald Scholarship. That is a grant of money for a very good student. Now life got a little easier for Charles. He could even afford to go out to eat once in a while.

Charles liked living in Canada because black and white people mixed together. It was not like being in Washington, D.C., where people of different races did not do things together. Charles began to make friends in Canada. Some of his friends were white, and some were black. He liked them all,

Charles was in a special group of top students at McGill Medical School.

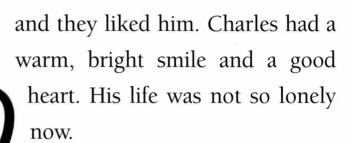

and they liked him. Charles had a warm, bright smile and a good heart. His life was not so lonely now.

Sometimes Charles and his friends went to a special little restaurant in Montreal. Charles liked to order a dish called pigs knuckles. It tasted like crispy fried pork chops.

In 1933, Charles graduated from McGill Medical School. He had the second highest grades of all the students. Charles felt very good about his success.

When a doctor finishes medical school, the next step is to learn more by working in a hospital under other doctors. For two years, Charles worked at hospitals in Montreal. He became a fine surgeon.

Next, he had to work and study in a hospital in the United States. But white hospitals did not want black doctors caring for their patients. Charles was turned down many times. At last, he was accepted to Howard University in Washington, D.C. He would teach medical students and do surgery at Freedmen's Hospital. Charles would be near his family, too. His father had recently died. His mother would be glad to have him close by.

Charles, center, worked with medical students at Howard University.

Chapter 3

Healing the Sick

A t Howard University and Freedmen's Hospital, Charles proved that he was smart and talented. The older doctors could see that Charles was special.

In 1938, Charles won a Rockefeller Fellowship. This is a grant of money to pay for more education. Charles was accepted to Columbia University Medical School for advanced training in surgery.

Some of the doctors Charles worked with at

Columbia were world-famous. One of them was Dr. John Scudder. He was an expert in the use of blood to save lives.

No black doctor had ever been trained at Columbia University Medical School and its Presbyterian Hospital. There were many black patients, but black doctors had never been allowed to work there. Charles changed all that. He was a good doctor, and he had a warm, friendly way. His patients and the other doctors liked him and trusted

At Columbia, Charles learned all about blood.

him. The color of his skin did not matter to them.

In 1939, Charles went to Alabama to spend some time at a health clinic for sick people who had no money for doctors. On his way there, Charles visited friends in Atlanta. That was where he met Lenore Robbins, a teacher. Charles and Lenore were married on September 23, 1939. Over the years they would have four children: Roberta (called Bebe), Charlene, Rhea, and Charles Jr.

In June 1940, Charles was awarded a doctor of medical science degree from Columbia University. He was the first African American to earn this degree.

At Columbia, Charles had studied how blood can save lives. When people lose blood in accidents or by sickness, other blood can be pumped back into their bodies. This is called a blood transfusion.

Charles also studied different ways of

The Drew family at home. From left: Rhea, Charles, Charlene, Bebe, Lenore, and baby Charles Jr.

storing blood. It is very important to have blood ready when people need it. The places of storage are called blood banks. Charles discovered that blood could be stored longer if the red blood cells were separated from the plasma. The plasma is the liquid part of the blood. Charles found that plasma was better for storing and for transfusions.

Because of all his study, Charles knew more about using blood to help people than almost anyone else.

Chapter 4

Blood to Save Lives

During World War II, which had begun in 1939, Charles was offered an important new job. In Europe, many people were being hurt and killed in the war. Bombs rained down in Great Britain. Thousands of people needed blood transfusions to stay alive. Britain did not have enough blood, so it turned to the United States for help. Charles was asked to head the Blood for Britain program.

Charles invented a fast, safe way to get blood quickly to the injured people of Britain. He set up places where Americans could donate blood. When the American people found out how much their blood was needed, they lined up to donate blood.

Charles, left, started the first blood bank on wheels. He used an ambulance.

Blood is stored until a sick person needs it.

Charles set up places where the blood could be stored. These were the blood banks he knew so much about.

He also arranged for the blood to be checked and double-checked. It had to be free of germs. If any deadly germs were in the blood, the transfusion could kill the person who received it.

Charles did an excellent job of quickly sending blood to Britain. Thousands of lives were saved. Because of his work in heading the Blood for Britain program, there was now a good way to move blood to those who needed it. After that, in times of war or natural disasters, people followed Dr. Drew's plan. He had come up with a way for blood to be safely collected, stored, and quickly given to people.

Blood had been donated by white and black Americans for Britain. Today we know that all blood is the same. But at that time, some people said the blood from black donors must be kept separate.

Britain made posters asking people to donate blood.

They thought white people should not get blood from a black person. This was wrong, and it made Charles very sad.

Chapter 5

Teacher and Leader

Next, Charles set up a blood system in the United States. He worked for the American Red Cross, collecting blood that might be needed for American soldiers. The Red Cross did not want blood from African Americans. This made Charles angry.

He went back to work at Howard University and Freedmen's Hospital. There he trained young black doctors. He wanted them to be treated as well as white doctors. He wanted them to be the best. Charles said this was his most important work of all.

Charles was very famous by this time. He could have made a lot of money working for a big company. But he cared more about people than about money. He became the head doctor at Freedmen's Hospital.

Charles and his blood bank workers.

Charles often worked sixteen hours a day. He did not smoke or drink. He would not even use bad words. He told his students to follow in his path. He told them to be good and kind and to become the best doctors they could.

Charles knew that black doctors had a tough time. Many hospitals still would not let black doctors in to

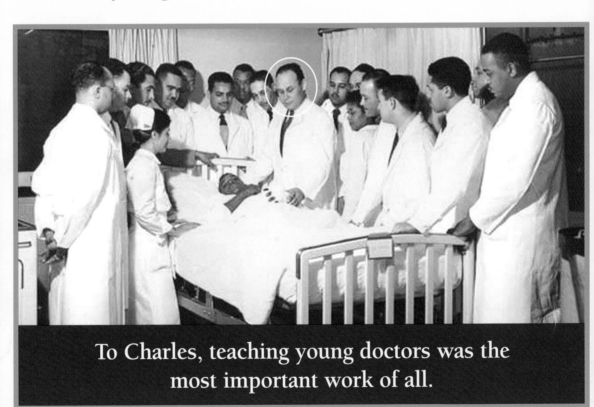

To Charles, teaching young doctors was the most important work of all.

care for patients. But Charles told them never to give up—just as he had never given up.

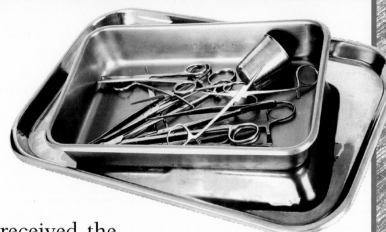

In 1944, Charles received the Spingarn Medal from the National Association for the Advancement of Colored People (NAACP). This important award is given to an outstanding black person every year.

For Charles, an even bigger moment was just ahead. He had been training young black doctors and teaching them how to do surgery. Now they would be taking their tests. They would be competing with white doctors. Charles wanted his students to do well.

When the results came in, Charles was very happy. One of his students got the highest grade on the test, and another came in second. Charles jumped for joy.

Charles gave a speech just two days before his death.

Between 1941 and 1950, more than half of all new black surgeons in the United States were trained by Dr. Charles Drew. He saw his biggest dream come true. The black doctors he had taught were now at the top. They proved they were as good as any white doctor.

In April 1950, Charles headed down to Alabama again to treat poor people at the free clinic. This work was very important to him. But on the way to Alabama, Charles was killed in a car accident. He was only forty-five years old.

Charles was praised by people all over the world. He had invented a system to bring blood quickly to those in need. He added much to what doctors knew about blood banks. He also trained many fine black doctors.

Charles never let anybody stand in the way of his dreams. He worked hard to become a great doctor. Then he opened the door for other young doctors to follow.

The U.S. Postal Service honored Charles Drew with this stamp.

All over America there are schools named for Dr. Charles Drew. A postage stamp came out on his birthday in 1981 honoring his life. In Los Angeles, a great medical school has been named for him. In his short life, Dr. Charles Drew made a great difference for goodness in this world.

CHARLIE DREW WAS ONLY A YOUNGSTER IN GRAMMAR SCHOOL WHEN THOUSANDS OF AMERICAN DOUGHBOYS DIED IN THE LAST WAR BECAUSE OF LACK OF ADEQUATE BLOOD TRANSFUSION TECHNIQUES.

THIRTY-NINE YEAR OLD DR. DREW'S WORK IN STANDARDIZING THE PREPARATION OF BLOOD PLASMA, WILL SAVE THE LIVES OF COUNTLESS UNITED NATIONS FIGHTING MEN ON BATTLE FRONTS ALL OVER THE WORLD.

RANKED AMONG THE FIRST FIVE HURDLERS IN THE COUNTRY

ALL EASTERN HALFBACK

ALL AMERICA MENTION

MISSED THE OLYMPICS BY THE FLIP OF A COIN!!

Dr. Charles Richard Drew, M.D., C.M., Med. D.Sc.

PROFESSOR OF SURGERY, HOWARD UNIVERSITY, CHIEF SURGEON, FREEDMEN'S HOSPITAL, WASHINGTON, D.C.

RECOGNIZED AUTHORITY ON THE PREPARATION AND PRESERVATION OF BLOOD PLASMA, ~ MEDICAL DIRECTOR OF THE PLASMA FOR BRITAIN PROJECT, AND DIRECTOR OF THE FIRST RED CROSS BLOOD BANK SET UP FOR THE COLLECTION OF BLOOD AND PLASMA FOR THE AMERICAN ARMED FORCES.

OUTSTANDING DOCTOR ~ FAMOUS ATHLETE

ALONG WITH PAUL ROBESON, NED GOURDIN, RALPH METCALFE, JESSE OWENS, CHARLIE DREW WAS A GREAT COLLEGE ATHLETE ~ FOUR LETTER MAN AND TRACK CAPTAIN AT BOTH AMHERST AND McGILL. DESPITE HIS ACHIEVEMENTS IN MEDICINE, HE RECALLS HIS POST AS COACH AT MORGAN COLLEGE AS "THE BEST JOB I EVER DID!"

alston owi

"You can do anything you think you can," said Charles Drew.

28

Timeline

1904~Charles is born in Washington, D.C., on June 3.

1926~Graduates from Amherst College. Becomes a coach at Morgan College.

1933~Graduates from medical school at McGill University.

1935~Becomes a teacher at Howard University, Freedmen's Hospital.

1938~Wins Rockefeller Fellowship and enters Columbia University.

1939~Marries Lenore Robbins.

1940~Awarded doctor of science in medicine from Columbia University. Heads Blood for Britain Program.

1944~Receives Spingarn Medal from NAACP.

1950~Dies after a car accident.

Words to Know

American Red Cross—An organization that helps people in times of suffering, such as war, health emergencies, and disasters.

blood bank—A place where donated blood is stored.

blood donor—A person who gives blood to be transfused into another person.

clinic—A place where people can get medical care.

National Association for the Advancement of Colored People (NAACP)—An organization started to help all Americans gain equal rights under the law.

surgeon—A medical doctor who operates on patients.

transfusion—Taking blood from one person, the donor, and putting it into the body of another.

World War II—A war fought in Europe, North Africa, and Asia from 1939 to 1945.

Learn More

Jackson, Garnet N. *Charles Drew, Doctor.*
Modern Curriculum Press, 1994.

Stille, Darlene R. *The Circulatory System.*
Children's Press, 1997.

Turner, Glennette Tilly. *Take a Walk in Their Shoes: Biographies of Fourteen Outstanding African Americans.* Penguin Putnam Books for Young Readers, 1992.

Internet Addresses

Read about Charles Drew at these Web sites.

<http://www.blackinventor.com/pages/charlesdrew.html>

<http://www.princeton.edu/~mcbrown/display/charles_drew.html>

Index